Search-and-Rescue Dogs

by Jessica Rudolph

Consultant: Ann Wichmann
Search and Rescue Dogs of the United States
FEMA Canine Search Specialist (retired)

BEARPORT
PUBLISHING

New York, New York

Credits
Cover and Title Page, © Kyodo/Newscom; 4, © Hemera/Thinkstock; 4–5,
© blickwinkel/Alamy; 6–7, © Tierfotoagentur/Alamy; 8, © Tina Rencelj/Shutterstock;
8–9, © Stockbyte/Thinkstock; 10–11, © blickwinkel/Alamy; 12–13, © Reuters/China
Daily; 14–15, © Stringer/China; 16, © Jason Reed/Reuters/Corbis; 16–17, © Denver
Post via Getty Images; 18, © Michael Reichel/dpa/Corbis; 19, © blickwinkel/
Alamy; 20–21, © blickwinkel/Alamy; 22, © petographer/Alamy; 23TL, © Roger
Ressmeyer/Corbis; 23TC, © blickwinkel/Alamy; 23TR, © AFP/Getty Images; 23BL,
© Tina Rencelj/Shutterstock; 23BC, © blickwinkel/Alamy; 23BR, © Minerva Studio/
Shutterstock.

Publisher: Kenn Goin
Creative Director: Spencer Brinker
Design: Deborah Kaiser
Photo Researcher: We Research Pictures, LLC

Library of Congress Cataloging-in-Publication Data

Rudolph, Jessica, author.
  Search-and-rescue dogs / by Jessica Rudolph.
      pages cm. — (Bow-wow! Dog helpers)
  Audience: 5 to 8.
  Includes index.
  ISBN 978-1-62724-122-9 (library binding) — ISBN 1-62724-122-1 (library binding)
  1. Search dogs—Juvenile literature. 2. Rescue dogs—Juvenile literature. I. Title.
  SF428.73.R83 2014
  636.7'0886—dc23
                                                2013032377

For more information, write to Bearport Publishing Company, Inc., 45 West 21st Street, Suite 3B,
New York, New York 10010. Printed in the United States of America.

10 9 8 7 6 5 4 3 2

Contents

Meet a Search-and-Rescue Dog

I'm a **search-and-rescue dog.**

I help find missing people!

Woof! Woof!

A search dog works with a human partner. This person is called a handler.

Handler

Search-and-rescue dog

My handler takes me to the place where a person got lost.

Then I go to work!

Search dogs work day or night.

How do dogs like me find people?

We use our noses!

Some dogs can smell a person half a mile (0.8 km) away.

Search dogs look for people lost in the woods.

We sniff around to find the person's **scent**.

Then we follow it.

Some search dogs bark when they find someone. This tells the handler to come over.

Search dogs also look for missing people after a **disaster**.

We climb over buildings that fell down.

We sniff for people buried under **rubble**.

Disasters such as **tornadoes** destroy buildings.

After a dog finds someone, rescue workers uncover the person.

People who are hurt are brought to a hospital.

Dogs can smell a person buried under 30 feet (9 m) of rubble.

How do dogs learn
to find people?

As puppies, handlers
train us.

Search dogs learn to follow a person's smell.

We are taught to walk safely over rubble.

We learn to bark when we find someone.

Search dogs learn to walk through tunnels and climb ladders.

We love using our sniffing skills.

With our handlers' help, we save lives!

Search dogs get a **reward** when they do a good job.

Search-and-Rescue Dog Facts

- Instead of barking, some search dogs are taught to run back to their handlers when they find someone in the woods. Then they show the handler where the missing person is.

- Search dogs may wear vests to let others know they are working. Some handlers do not put vests on their dogs because the vests might get caught on rubble.

Glossary

disaster (duh-ZASS-tur) a sudden event that causes terrible damage or suffering

reward (ri-WARD) what one gets for doing something useful or good

rubble (RUHB-uhl) pieces of broken rock, bricks, and other building materials

scent (SENT) a smell

search-and-rescue dog (SURCH-AND-RES-kyoo DAWG) a dog that searches for people who are lost or trapped

tornadoes (tor-NAY-dohz) powerful spinning towers of air that move over land and can cause much destruction

Index

Read More

Engle, Margarita. *When You Wander: A Search-and-Rescue Dog Story.* New York: Henry Holt (2013).

Schuh, Mari. *Search and Rescue Dogs (Pebble Plus: Working Dogs).* Mankato, MN: Capstone (2011).

Learn More Online

To learn more about search-and-rescue dogs, visit **www.bearportpublishing.com/Bow-WOW!**

About the Author

Jessica Rudolph lives in Connecticut. She has edited and written many books about history, science, and nature for children.